# YOUR KNOWLEDGE HAS VALUE

Deborah Heinen

# Sign language acquisition of deaf children

GRIN Verlag

**Bibliografische Information der Deutschen Nationalbibliothek:**

Die Deutsche Bibliothek verzeichnet diese Publikation in der Deutschen National-
bibliografie; detaillierte bibliografische Daten sind im Internet über http://dnb.d-
nb.de/ abrufbar.

**Imprint:**

Copyright © 2012 GRIN Verlag GmbH
Druck und Bindung: Books on Demand GmbH, Norderstedt Germany
ISBN: 978-3-656-68819-8

**This book at GRIN:**

http://www.grin.com/en/e-book/275856/sign-language-acquisition-of-deaf-children

**GRIN - Your knowledge has value**

Der GRIN Verlag publiziert seit 1998 wissenschaftliche Arbeiten von Studenten, Hochschullehrern und anderen Akademikern als eBook und gedrucktes Buch. Die Verlagswebsite www.grin.com ist die ideale Plattform zur Veröffentlichung von Hausarbeiten, Abschlussarbeiten, wissenschaftlichen Aufsätzen, Dissertationen und Fachbüchern.

**Visit us on the internet:**

http://www.grin.com/

http://www.facebook.com/grincom

http://www.twitter.com/grin_com

Table of Contents:

1

# 1) Introduction:

Sign Language – an issue which is, for most people, a riddle wrapped up in an enigma. It is kind of mystic for people who have little or no relation to sign language or people practicing it. Those people wonder about how the communication system of signing people works and how the sign language acquisition develops. Even linguists who dealt with this topic were not in complete agreement. "Until about 1970, the linguistic status of sign language was regarded as highly controversial" (Rodda/Grove 1987:101), which is founded on many reasons. This term paper shall try to give answers on the questions mentioned above, occasionally beholding also the opposed views of several linguists on sundry topics. But first it has to be said that the issue of sign language and it´s acquisition is an enormous domain. Therefore only the basic information is given, so the reader can understand and follow the elementary process of sign language acquisition. Furthermore the reader needs to know that the stereotype in this exposition is a prelingually deaf child who is exposed to sign language, ostensibly American Sign Language, since his or her birth.

Giving a first impression of how the system of sign language works, this term paper starts off with the formal and grammatical structure of American Sign Language. Subsequent a comparison with the structure of British Sign Language follows, so the reader can get a picture of the similarities and differences between those two sign languages, which is kind of interesting because oral English in America and Britain differs essentially in spelling, but not in grammar. After this we will focus on the main part of this term paper, the acquisition of sign language in the deaf child. The development of "speech" is presented chronologically, so that it is easier for the reader to follow. Moreover, the direct comparison to language acquisition of hearing children is drawn in places and even a short essay of deaf children trying to use oral speech is given in this chapter. Therefore the reader is able to develop gradually an own impression of the issue. Then, in the next chapter, the vocabulary of hearing and deaf children is compared, which is also an interesting item, because there exist several different opinions in regard to this. The last chapter deals with the answer to the central questions of this term paper which are: How does the acquisition of sign language differ from language acquisition of hearing children? Are they therefore handicapped? If yes, to what extent?

This term paper is mainly based on six authors, who are in particular Michael Rodda, Carl Grove, Roland Pfau, Markus Steinbach, Bencie Woll and Anne Baker. These authors were depicted because thus one can see the development in linguistic research on this field due to the fact that Rodda and Grove published their findings in 1987, Baker and Woll in 2008 and Pfau,

2

Steinbach and Woll again in 2012, so there are three different periods in time which show chronologically their research developments and improvements in this issue.

The reason why people deal with the subject of deaf people and their way of communication is simply interest. Everything what is unknown by a human evokes interest, in this case it is especially the (sign) language acquisition in the deaf child, because it is a little more unfamiliar to us than communication of deaf adults. One wonders about how prelingually deaf children know how to communicate without understanding oral speech. A hearing person can´t imagine that one is able to "speak" without speech, but, regarding to this, this term paper might be able to smooth some misapprehensions out.

## 2) Sign language as a Language:

Most people who are not exposed to sign language or are not in contact with people practicing sign language do not understand the system of signing. In this chapter, there will be given a brief overview on that topic.

The issue of whether sign languages are "real" languages or not has been highly discussed for a long time. Non-verbal communication systems were thought to be "linguistically primitive, lacking in vocabulary, grammatically confused and incapable of expressing subtle and abstract concepts" (Rodda/Grove 1987:101). William Stokoe is considered as the originator of the acceptance American Sign Language being a real human language, basing his arguments on parallels found in grammatical structures in both, spoken and signed languages (cf. Liddell 2003:VIII). This research by Stokoe in 1960 brought the perception of sign languages being full, complex and independent human languages (cf. Pfau et al. 2012:1).

The first and most significant difference between spoken and signed languages seems to be about the communication channel. Spoken languages transmit information through vocal articulation, which get perceived by the ear. In contrast, sign languages transmit information by body movements, which get perceived visually. This difference is called "modality difference" (ibid.:2).

Finally, how does sign language work? The text, clumsily said, is carried by the hands, whereas intonation is produced by the upper face, for example by the brows and the eyelids, but this area of sign language research is not well enough explored yet (cf. ibid.:71). Signs which are made at the same part of the body often have a familiar meaning (cf. ibid.:79f). So signs that are made on the temple often have a meaning with reference to mental activity, for example remember, learn

3

and worry, whereas signs which are articulated on the chest often express feelings, like love, suffer or happy (cf. ibid.:79f).

What gives sign languages, in this case especially American Sign Language, a linguistic character is the use of so called cheremes, which are closely parallel to phonemes in spoken languages. Spoken English uses about 44 phonemes, whereas American Sign Language uses 55 major cheremes (cf. Rodda/Grove 1987:129).

Furthermore there are three basic parameters (by Stokoe) in American Sign Language (cf. ibid.:129):

1) Dez. This is the shape adopted by the signer´s hand(s) (cf. ibid.:129). In American Sign Language there are 19 handshapes (cf. ibid.:349). This parameter is, typically acquired the latest of the three major parameters by deaf children (cf. Pfau et al. 2012:655f).

2) Tab. This shows the location of the sign relative to the signer´s body (cf. Rodda/Grove 1987:129). American Sign Language contains 12 basic locations (cf. ibid.:349). Location is, in general, mastered earliest, produced accurately in even the first signs (cf. Pfau et al. 2012:655f).

3) Sig. This describes the motions made by the signer´s hand(s) during execution of a sign (cf. Rodda/Grove 1987:129) and there are about 24 different movements in American Sign Language (cf. ibid.:349). Movement is the parameter which gets acquired second by deaf children (cf. Pfau et al. 2012:655f). Sig is also the most complex sign parameter and can be subdivided into the following classes of movements: movements of the fingers or wrist, linear movements in one of the signing planes, circular movements, interactions of both hands, simultaneous clusters of basic movement components and sequential and/or simultaneous combinations of movement (cf. Rodda/Grove 1987:130).

In American Sign Language, 40% of the signs are made with only one hand, 35% with both hands and 25% are made with one active hand and a passive one, functioning as the basis for the active hand (cf. ibid.:129). Signs are articulated at: the forehead, cheek, mid-face, lips, chin, neck, trunk, upper arm, forearm, wrist, base hand and at the neutral space in front of the signer (cf. ibid.:130). In addition to that, American Sign Language has, like any oral language, a phonetic, gestural, phonemic, morphological, syntactical and semantic level (cf. ibid.:151). Also the internal structure is similar to that of spoken languages (cf. ibid.:154) and the formal structure is elaborated on a par with them (cf. ibid.:138). Taken all this together, it gets clear that American Sign Language is everything but not pantomimic as some would say. To give evidence about that, Klima and Bellugi conducted a test in 1979 with 10 hearing non-signing persons who should identify 90 signs of American Sign Language. Only nine signs out of 90 were identified correctly (cf. ibid.: 133).

Now we are turning to the grammatical aspects of American Sign Language. It has, for example, also a number system, like spoken languages normally have. Singular is articulated by movements that go straightforward and plural by dissipated movements to the side (cf. ibid.:144). An example: "MAN, ME ASK" (meaning "I asked the man/men") can be articulated with a movement going straightforward, meaning one man, or with a dissipated movement to the side, meaning several men, but the location where the movement is made stays the same in both varieties (cf. ibid.:144).

In American Sign Language, like in spoken English, nouns and verbs are often very related. They only differ in the manner of movement. Nouns are articulated with the same motion, but in a more restrained manner (cf. ibid.:145). They can also be transformed into adjectives, for example "China-Chinese", by using a faster and more fraught movement (cf. ibid.:145). The action of a verb is shown by movements leading towards or away from specifically allotted location in the signing space (cf. .:149). Verb inflections are split, some are obligatory, some are optional (cf. ibid.:144). Most natural languages mark inflection by using sequential realignment of morphemes, whereas American Sign Language uses simultaneous inflections (cf. ibid.:139f). That means that a basic sign structure is attached in a complex sample of motions which systematically modify it´s meaning (cf. ibid.:139f). For example the sentence "Three of them came over to me" can be subdued into one single inflected sign of American Sign Language (cf. ibid.:139f). In addition to that, verbs in American Sign Language are sometimes transitive and need an obligatory indexing component (cf. ibid.:149).

Tense marking is a quite difficult issue in sign language. In American Sign Language, tense is articulated by time adverbials and movements differing in length (cf. Pfau et al. 2012:189). So, when the signer wants to express past with adverbials like "yesterday" or "before", he or she makes movements proceeding backwards, whereas in adverbials referring to the future the movements is made forward into neutral signing space (cf. ibid.:189). As mentioned before, the distance in time is indicated by the length of movement (cf. ibid.:189). Present tense is expressed by movements in front of the signer´s body (cf. ibid.:189).

Moreover, there are some differences regarding to spoken English pointed out by Rodda and Grove. They are of the opinion that sign order does not follow "normal word sequence", that signs are insufficient for certain parts of speech and therefor conclude that American Sign Language does not reflect the syntactical structures of spoken English (cf. Rodda/Grove 1987:102).

## 3) A Comparison Between American And British Sign Language :


The first systematic studies on British Sign Language came up about the 1970s (cf. ibid.:347), that is to say about 10 years after the study of American Sign Language found it´s beginning. Moreover British Sign Language has not been subjected to as intensely a program of research as that one of American Sign Language, which is studied well by the Salk Institute´s long-term study (cf. ibid.:353). The correspondent to William Stokoe in American Sign Language research is incarnated by Margaret Duchar, an independent researcher, for British Sign Language. According to Rodda and Grove, British Sign Language is harder to study than the American one, because the boundaries of sign and gesture, syntax and morphology, and linguistic against paralinguistic elements are difficult to define (cf. ibid.:354).

First we will focus on the similarities between the two of them. British Sign Language is, as well as American Sign Language, an incorporating language, because it compresses plenty of information into a "spatially and temporally complex matrix of formational features" (ibid.:353). Also the spatial process is exploited by British Sign Language to the full with the same mechanisms like in American Sign Language (cf. ibid.:353). Therefor it is used the modulation of basic signs, a limited set of formational elements, spatial deictic processes, and size and shape specification (cf. ibid.:353).

The differences between both sign languages are much more variegated. The first thing that distinguishes British Sign Language from American Sign Language is referred to the basic parameters. Compared to the parameters of American Sign Language, which are explained above, British Sign Language contains 17 basic locations, 18 handshapes and 25 types of movement (cf. ibid.:348). But it also consists of two more parameters, one called "Ori" for orientation, referring to the relation between palm and fingers, and the second called "secondary location", describing the points of contact between the hands (cf. ibid.:349).

Tense in British Sign Language follows a different pattern as in the American one, in which the idea of different locations stays the same. The system contains four different locations, called time lines, and a variety of manual and nonmanual adjuncts (cf. ibid.:350). Time line one is located over the signer´s right shoulder and expresses past (cf. ibid.:350). The tense is usually indicated before the subject (cf. ibid.:350). The second time line is located above the left arm and expresses attributes referring to distance in time, duration and others, for example it stands for calender units (cf. ibid.:350). Time line three illustrates continuity and is located above the midriff (cf. ibid.:350). The last time line is located beyond the right side of the signer and expresses gradual change, the sign "year" for example can with the appropriate movements stand for several meanings like "yearly" or "five years ago" (cf. ibid.:350).

Furthermore British Sign Language contains no articles and it´s pronoun system differs basically from that of spoken English, because it differentiates just between singular and plural, for example "you" as singular form and "you" as plural form, but not between subject and object, for example "I" as a subject and "me" as an object (cf. ibid.:349).

In general, British Sign Language seems to be less restricted regarding to signing space and feature combination than American Sign Language and it seems not to follow the same symmetry constraints (cf. ibid.:353f). In addition to that it also seems to be more permissive of mimetic enlargement to formal signing (cf. ibid.:353f).

In conclusion, it is difficult to decide which of the two sign languages just presented is the more developed one. One could suggest that British Sign Language is less developed because it is also less researched and the system is not as latent as that of American Sign Language and furthermore American Sign Language is more widely spread than the British. The differences in facial expressions for example, which I did not mention above, can also be explained by the cultural backgrounds, because the British are, traditionally, less facially expressive than Americans, therefor they may have a correspondingly greater free capacity for facial coding (cf. ibid.:354).

But however, there is no clear and effective adjudgement to this question, one can only suggest.

## 4) The Development of Speech in Deaf Children:

Hearing children learn speech basically by imitating what they hear in their surroundings. But what about children who are unable to hear, especially prelingual deaf babies, and how does their mental lexicon develop? How do they communicate and is their way of communication comparable to the system of oral speech? It is very difficult to give a general answer to these questions ;but in the following it is tried to give a model of language acquisition of deaf children who are exposed to sign language and choose this way of communication, not the oral one. So the stereotype in this work is prelingually deaf and learns sign language as his or her first language.

First it has to be said that the linguistic base of sign language, which operates in a visual-spatial framework, seems to be rooted in the standard left hemisphere neural structures as well as that of spoken languages (cf. Rodda/Grove 1987:287). But it is difficult to determine definitely where sign language is located in the brain compared to spoken language, therefore test results are ambiguous (cf. ibid.:287). However, this can lead to the assumption that there are no differences in the neural mechanisms regarding to signed and spoken languages, which can lead again to the suggestion that spoken and signed languages are acquired, from the neurological view, nearly the same way.

Before hearing infants start speaking they communicate by so called "babbling". A related system to that can be recognized in the first steps of communication by deaf children. Petitto and Marentette (1991) found out that deaf babies start manual babbling nearly the same time like hearing babies start syllabic babbling (cf. Pfau et al. 2012:27). So this means that the babies repeat specific hand and arm movements which they see frequently. This period during their first nine months of life ends usually in their first sign (subject to the condition that they are exposed to sign language) at about one year of age like the first word in hearing babies (cf. ibid.:28). Petitto and Martenette conducted an experiment in 1991 with two deaf infants exposed to ASL from birth and three hearing infants to study their movements of the hand. There they came to the conclusion that this "manual babbling shared the phonetic and syllabic (movement) structure of natural sign languages and exhibited the repetitive, rhythmic patterns typical of vocal babbling" (cf. ibid.:649). Furthermore they found out that the babies' speech development followed the same time course documented for hearing babies including the syllabic babbling stage and the variegated babbling stage (cf. ibid.:649). But whereas some linguists are of the opinion that manual babbling follows the same pattern as syllabic babbling the others who are convinced of the opposite like Rodda/Grove (1987:232) are certain that deafness affects even this prelingual nonverbal communication system, especially if the parents are no native signers (cf. ibid.:232).

Between nine months and one year the deaf babies start pointing to self and other people as well as objects, but these gestures can´t be seen as linguistic actions yet (cf. Baker/Woll 2008:41f). Petitto reported 1987 on pointing behaviors of two 6 months old deaf girls with the result that these mentioned non-linguistic gestures referring to people were replaced by lexical signs in between 12 and 18 months (cf. Pfau et al. 2012:667). So one can come to the conclusion that infants are able to use pronouns at this age, but as a matter of course they make mistakes frequently. It seems to be most difficult for the babies to distinguish between self from other people which can also be recognized in the development of language acquisition in hearing infants until the age of three (cf. Rodda/Grove 1987:148). But for deaf children it is probably even more difficult because it is hard for them to build self-identity without being able to ask how they can relate themselves to others (cf. ibid.:18). Petitto conducted a test on the theme of pronouns with hearing and deaf babies which displayed great difficulties for the infants to choose the right pronoun to relate to themselves. Most times they signed or understood "you" or "yours" instead of "I", "me" and "myself" ( cf. Pfau et al.2012:667). He came to the conclusion that "the full pronoun system was not mastered until around 27 months" (cf. ibid.:667) and that the acquisition of pronouns by the deaf subjects showed similarities to the development of pronouns in speaking children in time course and kinds of mistakes (cf. ibid.:667). This experiment is the only one made for the theme of pronouns but its results are however admitted (cf. ibid.:667).

Furthermore, deaf children have to make sure that their environment understands their gestures, so there has to be a high degree of transparency and they prefer naturally highly iconic forms (cf. ibid.:651). Meier et al. found out in 2008 that the also signing adults of 8-17 months old deaf signing children rated nearly 60% of the signs produced by their kids as neither more nor less iconic that their target forms (cf. ibid.:651). Nevertheless iconicity seems not to be a significant factor in sign acquisition (cf. Rodda/Grove 1987:363).

At about one year of age, as mentioned before, deaf babies exposed to sign language produce their first sign. From that moment on their vocabulary grows constantly in contrast to speaking/hearing children who sample a vocabulary burst in their first three years (cf. Pfau et al.:661). The first signs seem to be arranged around semantic categories which are comparable to the first words learned by children of any language (cf. ibid.:659f). Fenson conducted an experiment in 1994 with 69 children exposed to American Sign Language and reported that most of the first signs produced by them were nouns and dealt with themes like family, food, animals, clothing and greetings (cf. ibid.:659f). At the end of the experiment Fenson concluded referring to his data that the process and period of acquisition of other signs like wh-signs, negative signs, emotion signs or two-sign combinations is suitable to the standards of spoken American English (cf. ibid.:659f). A common mistake in the first signs is often over-generalization, for example is the term "car" used for every wheeled vehicle (cf. Baker/Woll 2008:41f).

To establish a connection to the language development of hearing and speaking children it is worth mentioning an experiment, conducted by Bonvillan, Orlansky and Novack in 1983. The persons tested were hearing children aged one to two years with deaf parents. They found out that these children produced their first sign at the age of 8 ½ months, whereas the first word is produced typically aged between 11-14 months. Also the first sign combination was produced at the age of 17 months, the first word combination is usually produced aged 18-21 months. These results let them suggest that "signs are easier to produce than words" (Rodda/Grove 1987:363), also because parents are able to guide their children more directly in their gestures. In addition to that Bonvillan, Orlansky and Novack reasond because of their data that motor activity in a child develops faster than the speech system (cf. ibid.:363).

After the first signs are generally nouns, the acquisition of verbs finally starts at the age of 1 ½ –

2 years (cf. Baker/Woll 2008:41f). The first verbs of sign-exposed children appear usually without productive verb morphology, that means for example that there are no subjects or objects used with agreement verbs, so there is also no morphological differentiation between verbs and nouns (cf. ibid.:41f). This distinction occurs first at about two or three years (cf. Rodda/Grove 1987:149). Ivimey conducted an experiment in 1981 on verb development in deaf children. There he ascertained three stages of verb acquisition. First of all deaf children start with the usage of unit verbs, "a verb form combined with external markers indicative of tense, rather than the appropriate inflections or auxiliaries" (cf. ibid.:175). On the second stage children learn how to use the right verb forms to mark future, while unit verbs are still kept for past and present. Finally on the third stage, at about the age of 14, deaf children are able to use the correct verb forms for all three times, but there is no form used for third person singular (cf. ibid.:175). Quigley, Montanelli and Wilbur found out in 1976 that there are four typical errors made by deaf children in handling verbs, which are about the usage of auxiliaries, inflections and copulas, and sometimes even the elision of a verb (cf. ibid.:174). These errors might lead to mistakes of comprehension. For example: To tell someone "you give me", the verb "give" has to be inflicted. If it is not inflicted, the utterance will turn its meaning to "I give you" (cf. ibid.: 149). Between two and three years of age, the children learn to use the correct form, which can lead to the conclusion that they are able to learn the rules of language even with irregular forms. A Salk Institute´s ASL research resulted in the awareness that attempts by parents of deaf children to correct their ASL grammar through direct guidance of his or her hands was without any effect, which leads to the suggestion that children have an internal rule-governed system of language acquisition (cf. ibid.:118).

Between 1 ½ and 2 year there appear also the first two-sign utterances (cf. Baker/Woll 2008:41f.). But whereas adults use sign order grammatically, e.g. for marking inflections, signing children use it just for pointing out semantic relations (cf. ibid.:41f.).

At about the age of two, children communicating with signs start, as we have slightly seen above, developing morphology and syntax (cf. Pfau et al. 2012:661). Regarding again to the pronouns one can recognize that at the age of 2 ½ , first, second and third person are correctly differentiated. The pronoun system is, according to the Salk Institute´s ASL research, fully acquired at the age of 2 years and 3 months (cf. Rodda/Grove 1987:118). Children are now also able to make the first distinctions between nouns and verbs (cf. Baker/Woll 2005:41f). Furthermore the first active use of verb agreement appears at this age (cf. ibid.:41f). This leads to the conclusion that deaf children learn the syntactical rules of language earlier than the morphological ones. According to Chen Pinchler (2001), they have also acquired the canonical word order rules by 30 months of age (cf. Pfau et al. 2012:663).

At three years of age, deaf infants are able to inflect verbs either for movement or manner, but they are not yet able to combine both (cf. Baker/Woll 2008:41f). That means for example if movement shows an inflection, manner is signaled separately from the verb in a continuous way (cf. ibid.:41f). Deaf children learn the correct and coordinated usage approximately half a year later (cf. ibid.:41f). The greatest development on this stage is the correct use of number morphemes (cf. ibid.:41f), but also the ability to construe new verb forms from nouns and are now also able to learn the morphological rules in irregular sign language forms (cf. Rodda/Grove 1987:150).

Day conducted an experiment in 1982 about the mother and deaf child interaction with 35 - 43 old deaf babies using primarily one- and two-sign utterances. The result:

a) 26,8% were descriptions, most events, identity and locations.

b) 20,2 % were requests. The children asked their mothers most times to do something or about an object. Wh-questiones and Yes-/No-questiones were slightly emerging.

c) 18,2% consisted of controversial devices, for example checks, comments, offers, polite responses or requests.

d) 15,5% were responses.

e) 16% were statements and performances, that means "nonformal and formal linguistic expressions and sensomotoric activities (cf. ibid.:232f).

With five years the capability of most morphology is completed and used correct most of the time (cf. ibid.:41f). In the following four years, the development of requirements of narration is ongoing and enhanced, because while most structural elements at the sentence level are completely acquired, the grammatical elements are still lacking referring e.g. to cohesion, narrative role and sentence conjunction (cf. ibid..41f).

At about the age of 10, have finally learned the noun phrase + verb phrase construction, which is acquired by hearing children normally at the age of 2 (cf. Rodda/Grove 1987: 173). Before this acquisition of the noun phrase + verb phrase construction, a sentence like "The cat chases the dog" might be interpreted the other way around because this situation is more common (cf. ibid.:173).

Sentence conjunctions, for example with "and", "or" and "but", are acquired until the age of three by hearing children, but deaf children have great difficulties in using these conjunctions correctly, so they make a number of characteristic mistakes (cf. ibid.:173). Two of these errors are for example the omission of an object word from the second conjoined sentence or the omission of the subject from a second sentence (cf. ibid.:173). Referring to this a typical sentence might be: "The boy saw the turtles and ate the fish", whereas he or she would be wanting to say that the turtles were eating the fish (cf. ibid.:173). At the age of 18, only 80% of these sentence conjunctions are used correctly by deaf persons (cf. ibid.:173).

Tweney, Hoemann and Andrews invented in 1975 a test for the analysis of the semantic organization in the brain of deaf adolescents compared to hearing ones (cf. ibid.:163). The 63 hearing subjects and the 63 deaf, aged between 16 and 18, should place common nouns and words relating to sounds in the correct categories. Regarding to the common nouns, deaf and hearing subjects rated nearly the same degree of semantic consistency and referring to the sound words, the deaf subjects were only slightly less consistent, by putting the sound words frequently in a "Don´t know" category, than the hearing subjects (cf. ibid.:163).

All these things explained above are alluding to prelingually deaf children who choose sign language as their way of communication. But what about deaf children who try to use a spoken language? Several studies, experiments and tests produced the result that these children often have arrhythmic, monotonous, lacking in rhythm and pitch, containing poor paraphrasing speech (cf. ibid.: 24). Also the speech rhythm can be distorted, for example stuttering (cf. ibid.: 20). Furthermore there can be voice disorders, so called dysphonias, like speaking to loud, to low or without accentuation (cf. ibid.:20). Rodda and Grove are of the opinion that it is more effective to support the natural speech development in deaf children than to support speech itself (cf. ibid.: 19). Later on, when speech development has finished and the oral speech has become a sensible way of communication, specific oral inaccuracies should be corrected (cf. ibid.:19). Some of these inaccuracies are the following:

a) substitutions like "wock" for "rock". These substitutions are similar to those by babies, so they are also called "baby talk" (cf. ibid.:20).

b) omissions like "low" for "blow" (cf. ibid.:20).

c) additions like "buhlue" for "blue" (cf. ibid.:20).

d) distortions like "scweam" for "scream" (cf. ibid.:20).

e) lulling, which means that r, l, t, d and s sounds can be defective (cf. ibid.:20).

f) lisping, which refers to problems with s and z sounds (cf. ibid.:20).

g) delayed speech, which means that the child uses narrow range of consonants what leads to an unintelligible speech (cf. ibid..:20).

All these inaccuracies are common for deaf children trying to use oral speech, so one can argue whether sign language would be a better way of communication or not.


## 5) The Vocabulary - A Comparison Between Deaf And Hearing Children:

The theme of vocabulary of deaf and hearing infants is very controversial and highly discussed. One would, of course, suppose that the vocabulary of a prelingually deaf person is much smaller than that one of a hearing person, because of many factors. First of all hearing and speaking children can ask their environment about words they don´t know or don´t understand and their counterpart can give them an adequate answer in a suitable communication system. Deaf infants, however, need to paraphrase their request and have to find a solution to convert the information given to them in a suitable way. In the case of deaf infants there has to be, of course, a differentiation between deaf children with deaf parents and deaf children with hearing parents.
Baker and Woll are of the opinion, based on several studies, for example the one bye Kyle and Ackerman in 1990, that the vocabulary of deaf and signing children is larger during the first two years than the vocabulary of hearing and speaking children, but they also limit it by calling this phenomenon "transitory" (Baker/Woll 2008: 39f). One more study by Morgan and Woll from 2002 led to the conclusion that the vocabularies of children learning sing language have the same size as the ones of speaking children, because hearing children have a lexicon about 10 words at fifteen months and 50 words at twenty months, which is adequate to the results of the tests for deaf children (cf. ibid.:39f).
Another study led to a completely different result, which is that the vocabulary of a deaf infant is on the same level as the vocabulary of a six year old hearing and speaking child at the end of his or her school career (cf. Rodda/Grove 1987:165). This experiment was conducted by Silverman-Dresner and Juilfoyle in 1972, with 13.000 deaf children aged between 8 and 17. Silverman-Dresner and Juilfoyle gave a multiple choice test to the subjects with a list of words known generally by hearing children aged between 6 and 11. Now they should cross the words they

know. The result: The subjects aged between 8 and 9 knew only 18 words of 7300, which comes up to 0,25%, and the 16 to 17 year old subjects knew 2545 words, which comes up to 35% (cf. ibid.:165).

A different study by Myklebust seems to confirm the results by Silverman-Dresner and Juilfoyle. He analyzed the vocabulary in essays by deaf students and found out that they used much less verbs, pronouns, adjectives and adverbs than hearing children, but much more nouns (cf. ibid.:172).

Maybe the study by Marshark and Everhard in 1999 gives a possible solution on the question why deaf children´s vocabulary is much less developed than that of hearing children. Marshark and Everhard conducted an experiment with deaf and hearing children aged between seven and college age. They were shown a matrix consisting of 42 images including different things from different categories, for example a dog which refers to the category of animals. The subjects should ask 20 questions to find out the appropriate categories. Marshark and Everhard found out that the hearing subjects achieved better results in all ages than the deaf subjects and concluded that the deaf either have a lower ability to associate or they only make use of it infrequently (cf. Marshark et al. 2004:51f).

So in conclusion the recent research on this subject is not developed sufficiently yet to give an appropriate answer to the question above.

# 6) Conclusion:

Taking everything together one might come fast to the conclusion that deaf children are not profoundly handicapped referring to their language acquisition compared to hearing children, because every difference between them is described so insignificantly. But in my opinion one has to differ between the scientific view and the social one, because linguistically seen deaf children might have the same abilities in language acquisition like hearing infants, but socially seen it is, for sure, much harder than it is described by the linguists. Also the grammar of sign languages is described by most linguists as "sufficient", which may be sufficient indeed, but sufficient is not the same like "manifold" or "sophisticated", which describes oral language appropriately. One can suggest that linguists compliment sign languages and their grammar, because they thought it was "non-linguistic" and "no real speech" for a long time, but now they are aware that it is a real language indeed, so they excessively emphasize every linguistic aspect.

In general, from the linguistic point of view one can conclude that the development of language acquisition in the deaf and the hearing child is rather similar and follow the same pattern. But this requires the same experiences in their environment, which means, for example, that they have parents who care for their children´s speech development. The only thing that differs should be the manner of communication to which they are exposed, sign language or oral language. This implies in consequence: If a deaf child is exposed very early to well developed sign language or the signer is experienced in signing, they have the same chances to reach language skills in sign language on a high level, just like hearing and speaking children. But the other way around, if children are not exposed to well mastered sign language, they are not able to reach the same language skills like hearing and speaking children. So in conclusion, the success of signing children in reaching proficiency in sign language is dependent on the conditions to which they are exposed in early childhood. Summarized it can be said that there are, according to the majority of linguists´opinions,  no severe differences, with few exceptions, in language acquisition between hearing and deaf children.

From the social point of view, I guess that there are many more differences than from the linguistic point of view. Deaf children might have the same progression of learning linguistic features but sign languages and their grammar in general are not as developed as oral languages, so deaf children might have to learn less features of speech than hearing children and it might be possible that therefor they stay in the same time space like the hearing subjects.

Dealing with this issues I got the impression of a not yet sufficiently researched area and that linguists have a very restricted perception referring to this subject. I can´t completely agree on the statement that deaf children follow exactly the same pattern as hearing children because there are still too many different opinions referring to this, even if the majority of linguists agrees with that statement.

But as we have seen, everything is partly bounded to the personal perception and I guess, there will be no clear answer until linguists come up with a generally admitted achievement. So finally it can be reasoned that there are no clear without ambiguity responses on the central questions, whether and how deaf children are handicapped in speech development.

# 7) Literature:

- Baker, Anne & Bencie Woll. 2008. *Sign Language Acquisition*. Amsterdam: Benjamins.
- Brentari, D. 2012. "Phonology." In: Pfau, R., Steinbach, M. & Woll, B. (ed) 2012, 21-54.
- Marshark, Marc, Carol Convertino, Cathy McEvoy & Allison Masteller. 2004. "Organization and Use of the Mental Lexicon by Deaf and Hearing Individuals" *American Annals of the Deaf* (1): 51-61.
- Meir, I. 2012. "Word classes and word formation." In: Pfau, R., Steinbach, M. & Woll, B. (ed) 2012, 77 – 111.
- Pfau, R., Steinbach, M. & Woll, B. 2012. "Tense, aspect, and modality." In: Pfau, R., Steinbach, M. & Woll, B. (ed) 2012, 186-203.
- Pfau, R., Steinbach, M. & Woll, B. (ed). 2012. *Sign Language. An International Handbook*. Berlin/Boston: de Gruyter Mouton.
- Pichler, D. C. 2012. "Acquisition." In: Pfau, R., Steinbach, M. & Woll, B. (ed) 2012, 647-686.
- Rodda, Michael & Carl Grove. 1987. *Language, Cognition and Deafness*. Hillsdale, N.J.: Erlbaum.
- Sandler, W. 2012. "Visual prosody." In: Pfau, R., Steinbach, M. & Woll, B. (ed) 2012, 55-76.

Lightning Source UK Ltd.
Milton Keynes UK
UKHW041233291121
394745UK00010B/715